MODEL
BUILDIN

ALSO BY HARVEY WEISS

The Gadget Book
Games and Puzzles You Can Make Yourself
How to Make Your Own Books
How to Run a Railroad:
   Everything You Need to Know about Model Trains
Model Airplanes and How to Build Them
Model Cars and Trucks and How to Build Them
Motors and Engines and How They Work
Ship Models and How to Build Them

MODEL BUILDINGS

And How to Make Them

by Harvey Weiss

Illustrated with photos and drawings by the author

Thomas Y. Crowell   New York

Many thanks are due the following people, who very generously permitted the use of their model buildings as illustrations in this book. The page number on which the illustration appears is given after the name. Models not otherwise credited are by the author. Christopher Barten, 37; Daniel Rothenberg, top and bottom, 38; Abraham Rothenberg, top, 13 and 46; Leah Greenwald, top, 47; Walter Einsel, bottom, 47, 82, 95; Mathew Morris, 76; Margaret I. McKinnickinnick, 77; John Weiss, 78; unknown Puerto Rican craftsman, 74; Molly Brody of Molly Brody Miniatures, 84, 85, 90, 93, 94; Charles Reid and Sarah Reid, 92.

LIBRARY OF CONGRESS CATALOGING IN PUBLICATION DATA
Weiss, Harvey.
    Model buildings and how to make them.
    1. Architectural models—Juvenile literature.
I. Title.
NA2790.W44 1979   720'.22'8   77–26597
ISBN 0–690–01341–8

FIRST EDITION

CONTENTS

INTRODUCTION

A model of a house or building is a small piece of the real world that you can make yourself. It is something that expresses your own ideas, something that you can own.

It is possible—but not very likely—that one day you'll be the owner of an eighteenth-century French château, or the proprietor of an elegant town house. But with a little time and effort, you can have a model of one of these structures, which is almost as much fun as owning the real thing!

All the model buildings described in this book are not that fancy, of course. You might prefer to build a model of a very simple little house in the country, the kind of house that you would like to live in someday. Or perhaps you would like to make a small version of the house in

Here's my cat Pushkin making a nuisance of himself, playing with my favorite model building.

which you now live, or in which a friend or relative of yours once lived.

Model buildings are also made by architects, so that they can visualize what the buildings they are planning will look like when they have actually constructed them. Some of these models are built by professional model builders and are made with great care and attention to detail. They are an important part of any architect's job.

Another kind of model building is the reproduction of famous or historically interesting monuments and buildings, such as the Taj Mahal or Thomas Jefferson's Monticello or an Egyptian tomb, for example.

Model buildings are also an important part of the model railroader's world. Once a model railroad gets beyond the going-around-in-a-circle sort of operation, there is a need for stations, factories, buildings of all kinds. This will give to the model railroad a lot of realism.

But for most people a model building is fun to make because the result is simply a beautiful object that is nice to have around, just as a good painting or a good piece of sculpture is nice to have around. As I write this, I can look up and see a small pink-and-brown town house sitting on a corner of my desk. It doesn't have any practical purpose. In fact, it is always in the way. I have to dust it every once in a while, and make sure the cat doesn't start playing with it. But every time I glance at it, I get a feeling of pleasure and satisfaction. I designed it; I built it. I like to look at it, and I'm proud of it. I wouldn't dream of storing it away in a closet or, heaven forbid, getting rid of it!

MODEL BUILDINGS OF CARDBOARD

1. USING CARDBOARD

Cardboard is an excellent material for making model buildings because it is simple to work with; it is cheap and easy to get. Cardboard isn't as strong or as good-looking as wood, but if the finished model is handled with reasonable care, it will last as long as you want it to.

WHAT KIND OF CARDBOARD?

Shirt Cardboard   This is the kind of cardboard that is found inside shirts that have been sent to a commercial laundry. It is used to keep the shirts from getting wrinkled. Shirt cardboard is not too stiff or too strong, but it is quite suitable for any model that isn't unusually large.

This house is made from cardboard. Lightweight cardboard is ideal for all sorts of model buildings.

Cardboard From Packages And Boxes   A shoe box, for example, will provide enough material for a small model house. The printing that covers the outside of most such boxes and packages can be placed on the inside, or left to show if the colors and patterns are pleasing. Before you can use this kind of cardboard, however, you will have to cut through it at the corners and spread the box out flat.

Corrugated Cardboard   This material is very plentiful. It is not really cardboard, however. It is actually two layers of brown paper with a middle layer of rippled paper between, and it is best avoided! Corrugated cardboard is difficult to glue. The edges look sloppy; the surface is slightly rippled. You might use it if there was absolutely nothing else available. But you will get much nicer results with any of the other kinds of cardboard mentioned.

Chipboard   This is simply the name for heavyweight cardboard. It can be found as the backing on large drawing pads. It is also used to make cigar boxes and as the stiffening material in the covers of books. It comes in different thicknesses. The very heavy kind is too difficult to cut, but the lightweight is ideal for all sorts of buildings. You can buy a 30-inch by 40-inch piece of chipboard at most art or stationery stores.

Other Kinds Of Cardboard   Art and stationery stores carry many other types of cardboard that can be used for model buildings. These cardboards are often called by other names, however. There is something called mat board, which comes in many attractive colors and is nice to work with. There are also various kinds of illustration board, mounting board, heavy bristol board, poster board, and so on. All of these can be used as long as they are not too thin and flimsy nor too heavy to cut easily.

Avoid cardboards that have either a very rough grain or a pebbled surface, and board that is very smooth and shiny. In both these cases the glue won't hold very well.

HOW TO CUT CARDBOARD

The thinner varieties of cardboard can be cut with a pair of good, large, sharp scissors. You must first rule a straight line as a guide, and then very slowly and carefully cut along the line with the scissors.

Another, much better way to cut cardboard is with a sharp knife. An X-Acto knife is the kind that many

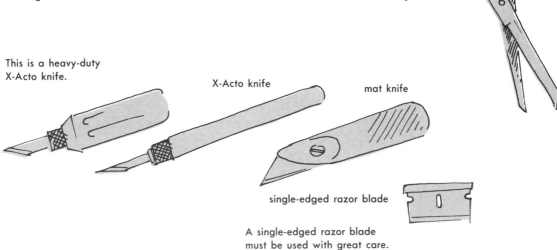

This is a heavy-duty
X-Acto knife.

X-Acto knife

mat knife

single-edged razor blade

A single-edged razor blade
must be used with great care.

model builders use. This sort of knife, which has a replaceable blade, costs a little more than a dollar at most art or hardware stores. A utility knife, or mat knife, is similar to an X-Acto knife. It is a little heavier and more rugged, and it also has a replaceable blade. A single-edged razor blade is another possible cutting tool, but it must be handled with the greatest care.

All these cutting tools should be used with a metal ruler as a guide. Otherwise it is very difficult to cut a straight line. A steel or aluminum ruler is ideal, but you can also use a wooden ruler if it has a metal edge. A plain wooden ruler won't work because the blade will snag in the wood. The way to use a knife and ruler is shown below.

Take your time! Don't try to cut right through the cardboard in one stroke. It may take two passes—or five or six passes—before the knife goes through the cardboard. It depends on how sharp the blade is and how thick the cardboard is.

Knife blades must be sharp. A dull blade is more dangerous than a sharp one because it is more liable to slip off in some unpredictable direction!

Put a piece of wood or an extra piece of cardboard under your work, or you will get cut marks on your table.

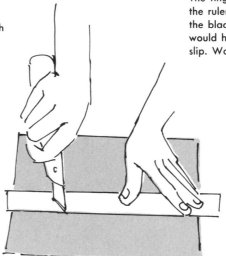

The fingers that are holding down the ruler should be well away from the blade. Always ask yourself what would happen if the knife should slip. Would it touch your fingers?

Press down hard on the ruler so it won't slip.

HOW TO BEND CARDBOARD

In order to give cardboard a sharp bend, such as when you are making the corner of a building, you must first *score* the cardboard. This means making a very shallow groove or indentation along the ruled line where the fold is to be. You do this by running a dull knife along the fold line. If you neglect to score the cardboard, the bend will be lumpy and sloppy. The score is made along the inside of the fold.

If you happen to be using a heavyweight cardboard, the scoring is done a little differently. In that case, a shallow cut is made with a sharp knife along the *outside* of the fold. The cut must, of course, go only partway through the cardboard.

MEASURING

Before any cardboard is cut, you must know *where* to cut it. This may seem pretty obvious. But it is actually the most important part of cardboard construction. The way you rule the lines that guide the cutting and folding will determine how neat your model will look and how easily it will fit together.

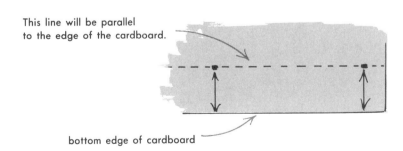

This line will be parallel to the edge of the cardboard.

bottom edge of cardboard

If you measure up from a straight edge in two places—and then rule a line between the two marks, you will have a line parallel to the edge. Don't ever trust your eye to draw one line parallel to another if you want any accuracy.

GLUING

Common white glue, such as Elmer's, is the best kind to use for cardboard construction. It is strong and dries fast. Another type sometimes used is fast-drying cement. This kind of cement comes in a tube and is often used to assemble plastic car or plane kits. What you should avoid, however, is rubber cement. It is neither strong nor permanent, and it is difficult to control.

A good deal of model-building construction involves the gluing of edges. If the edges to be joined come into straight and even contact, the glue will hold the parts together with a good deal of strength. Jagged and wavy edges will not hold, however, because too little of their surface areas touch.

If a piece of cardboard has a perfectly straight edge, it can be glued onto a flat surface and will stick securely. Not so, if the edge is bumpy and uneven.

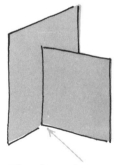

Glue along edge.

A stronger joint is made when one flat surface is glued onto another flat surface. There is more area for the glue to hold.

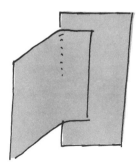

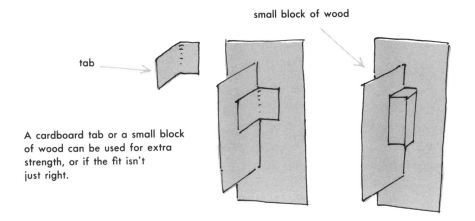

small block of wood

tab

A cardboard tab or a small block of wood can be used for extra strength, or if the fit isn't just right.

PAINTING

Most people like to leave their cardboard buildings unpainted. If the cardboard is clean and without stains, or if you have used one of the more fancy kinds of cardboard, there is no good reason to apply paint. If you do decide to use paints, almost any kind will do. Tempera or poster paints work fine. Acrylic artists colors are also excellent. Oil paints are all right, but take awhile to dry. If you do use oil-base paint, it is a good idea to give the cardboard a preliminary coat of shellac or varnish. This will keep the paint from soaking into the cardboard. Watercolors are not too good, because they are thin and transparent.

If you want to paint small details a different color from the rest of your building, it is wise to paint them before you glue them in place. This applies to things like shutters, window frames, door frames, chimneys, and so on.

2. GETTING STARTED

The small house shown here is about as simple as you can get. It is little more than a box with windows and doors—but it can be expanded into a much more elaborate building, as the next chapter will show.

It is strongly recommended, however, that you start your house-building career with this little structure, even if it seems somewhat too plain for your taste. While you are making this house and following the directions carefully, you will also be learning the various measuring and cutting methods you'll need when making more complicated buildings. The methods described here are used whether you are building a small cottage or a huge cathedral.

The size of this house is 4 inches wide by 6 inches long by 3½ inches high. This size was just picked at random; it is neither too large nor too small. There is, however, a

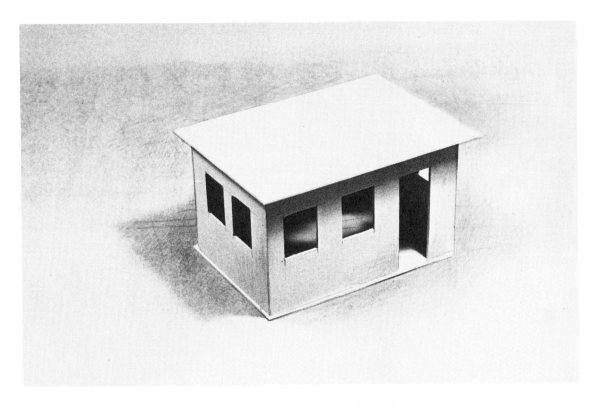

limit to the size of cardboard houses. Walls and roofs that are very large—especially if you are using thin cardboard—tend to bend and sag when they span large areas. Our 4-inch by 6-inch house can be built even from thin cardboard. This is the way to do it.

METHOD OF CONSTRUCTION

1. Measure up from the bottom of the cardboard 3½ inches as shown. Do this in two places, making a small pencil mark each time.

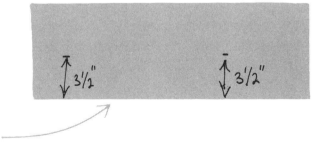

bottom edge of cardboard

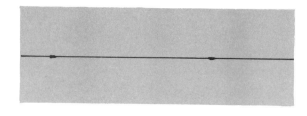

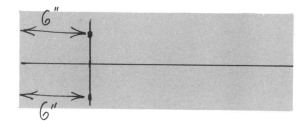

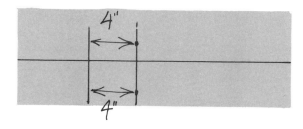

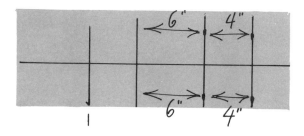

2. Using a ruler, draw a line connecting the two marks. This line is the height of the house walls.

3. Measure in 6 inches from the side. Do this in two places, making a small pencil mark each time. Connect the marks with a line. This line will be one corner of the house.

4. Measure in 4 inches from the line you've just drawn. Do this in two places, making a small pencil mark each time and connecting the marks, as before, with a line. This line will be the next corner of the house.

5. Repeat this operation twice more as shown, and you will have drawn all four walls of the house. Double-check to make sure all the lines are perpendicular and correctly spaced. (If the piece of cardboard you are working with isn't large enough, you will find that you can't place all four walls in a row as shown. In this case draw the front wall and a side wall. Then draw the back wall and the other side wall elsewhere on your cardboard.)

6. Now cut along the top, and the edge of the fourth wall.

7. Score the three vertical lines, which are to be the corners of the house. (Use a dull knife for the scoring, as explained in the previous chapter.)

Score along the dotted lines.

8. Now you can fold in the walls and get some idea of what your house is going to look like. But before you glue the edges together, lay the cardboard out flat again and plan where the windows and doors are to be.

9. Carefully rule in the position of these cutouts. Then cut along the lines with one of the knives already described. Windows and doors are tricky to cut out. You will have to make many light cuts with your blade until the cardboard comes free. Corners will need even a little more special care.

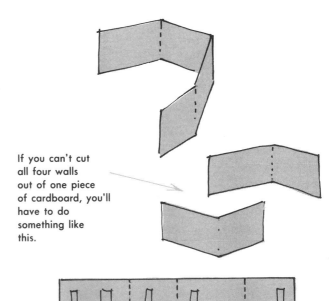

If you can't cut all four walls out of one piece of cardboard, you'll have to do something like this.

The position and size of the doors and windows is up to you.

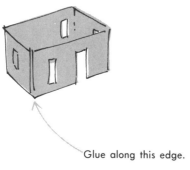

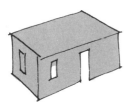

Glue along this edge.

10. Now run a thin bead of glue along one edge of the end wall. Join it to the other edge and hold the two pieces in place for a minute or two, until the glue dries. While you are doing this, make sure the bottoms of the walls are resting evenly on a flat surface. You don't want one side of your house to be higher than the other, or the building will wobble.

11. The final step is to cut out a flat piece of cardboard for the roof and glue it in place. Run the glue along the top edge of the house.

12. If the house seems a little less rigid than you'd like it to be, cut out another piece of cardboard to serve as a base to which the bottom of the walls can be glued.

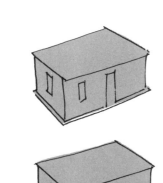

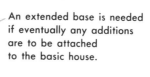

An extended base is needed if eventually any additions are to be attached to the basic house.

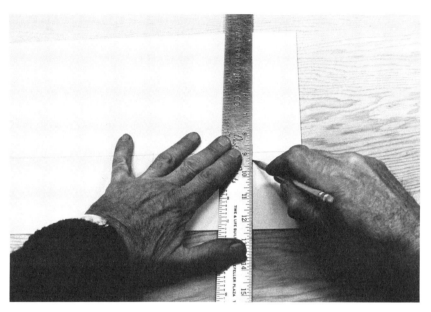

This photograph, and those that follow, show the key steps just described. This step, the measuring and ruling of the lines for cutting and scoring, is the most important of all.

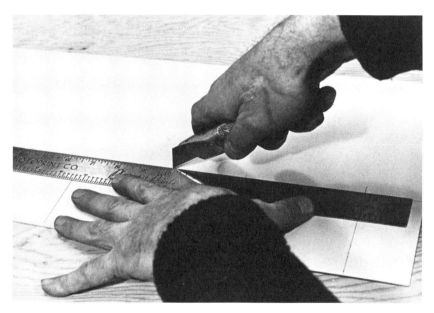

A mat knife is being used here for the cutting. Notice that the fingers are kept as far away as possible from the blade. Beginners find that the blade will sometimes wander away from the edge of the ruler. With a little practice on a few scraps of cardboard you'll learn to keep the blade traveling straight—right alongside the ruler.

In this photograph, a small, sharp-tipped X-Acto knife is being used to cut out the windows. This kind of cutting is slow and rather delicate and can't be rushed. You'll find that it takes a little extra effort to cut right up to the corners. A sharp knife is essential for this.

The walls are being held in place while the glue dries. The edges fitted together quite accurately in this little model. If they hadn't, a small block of wood or a cardboard tab would have provided some extra support.

Finally the roof is glued in place. The roof shown here has a rather large overhang, some of which was cut off when a second floor and a porch were added later on. The next step will be to cut out and attach a base, or bottom floor.

3. GETTING BIGGER AND BETTER

In this chapter we'll explore some of the different ways of adding on to the basic house described on the previous pages. The first improvement that comes to mind is a more interesting roof.

A PEAKED ROOF

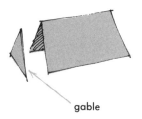

gable

This is made from one piece of cardboard that is scored, then folded down the center. In order for the roof to hold its shape, you'll need to insert a triangular piece at each end. Architects call such pieces gables. Cut out one gable, then use it as a pattern for marking and cutting the second. Glue both gables in place.

Here is the house from the previous chapter with a peaked roof, a second floor, a porch, a garage, a chimney, and other details added onto it.

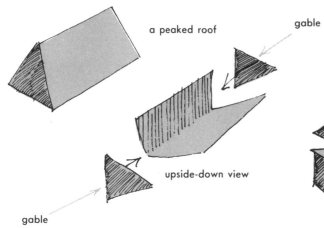

a peaked roof

gable

gable

upside-down view

If you want only a one-story house, but would like to add a peaked roof, you can do it like this. The flat roof of the original house will now be the attic floor!

The finished roof is simply glued onto the old flat roof.

A SECOND FLOOR

This is nothing more than a second house placed on top of the original one. If you want this addition to have a peaked roof, cut out the walls as shown in the drawing. In this case the triangular section, or gable, is part of the end walls.

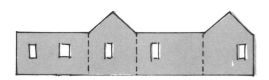

Here are the steps in making a second floor.

Glue in place.

Some peaked roofs are quite sharp.

Attach with glue.

The second floor (another little house) is in place on the flat roof of the original house.

A PORCH

A porch gets a bit more complicated because one end has to be supported by columns. The roof of the porch is a simple rectangle with side flaps. The columns can be made from whatever thin, sticklike material you can get your hands on. Lollipop sticks, Q-tips, stiff wire, twigs from trees or bushes, the wire from a wire coat hanger —any thin, straight material will do. You can also make the columns by gluing together two or three thin strips of cardboard, although they are apt to be a little flimsy. One of the best materials to use are applicator sticks. These are very thin wood rods. If you ask for some at a drugstore, the chances are the druggist will let you have a handful for nothing or for a few cents. They are very useful for all kinds of model making.

The floor of the porch is a rectangle of cardboard. If you are making a large porch, you will want one large piece of cardboard that will fit under the entire house.

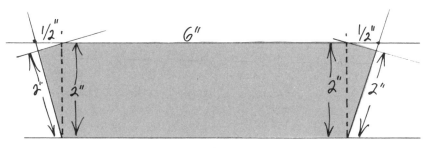

Here's how the porch roof and side panels can be cut out of one piece of cardboard.

Score along dotted lines.

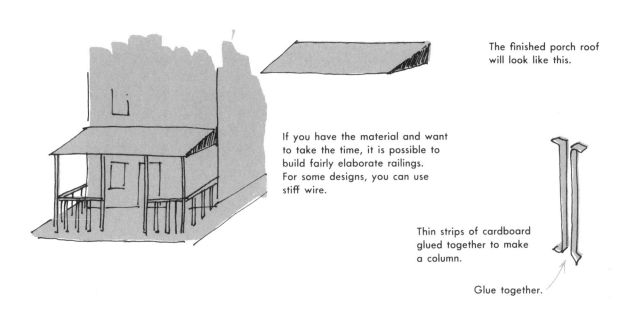

The finished porch roof will look like this.

If you have the material and want to take the time, it is possible to build fairly elaborate railings. For some designs, you can use stiff wire.

Thin strips of cardboard glued together to make a column.

Glue together.

A GARAGE

If this is to be attached to the house, you only need three walls. The roof of the garage can be either peaked or flat.

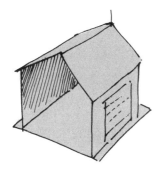

If the garage door is cut out and then attached on top of the opening with a piece of tape, you can get it to swing open.

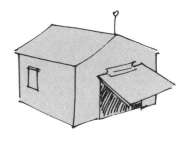

A CHIMNEY

Just about every house has a chimney, and even though it is a small addition, it is tricky to make because the bottom must be angled so as to fit on the roof. (On a flat roof you don't have this problem.)

Cut out a piece of scrap cardboard and experiment with it until you get the angles just right. Then trace the pattern onto the cardboard you are using for the actual chimney.

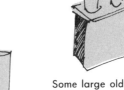

Some large old houses have chimneys that are fairly complicated.

THE LITTLE DETAILS

If you look closely at any real, full-size house, you will see many little additions. Some of these extra details, which help make a model house look more realistic, are shown here.

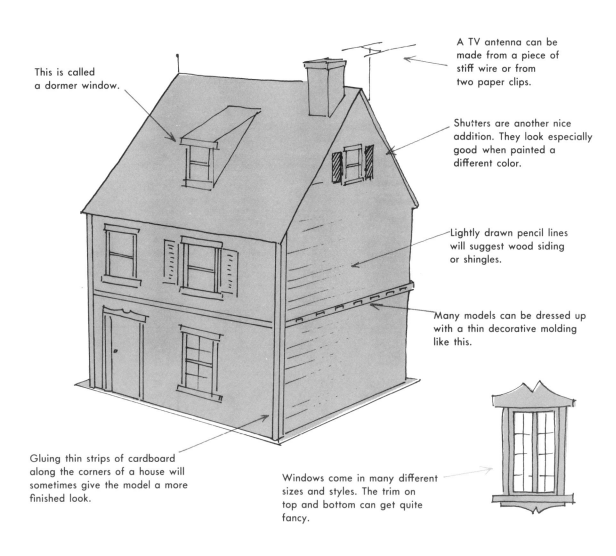

This is called a dormer window.

A TV antenna can be made from a piece of stiff wire or from two paper clips.

Shutters are another nice addition. They look especially good when painted a different color.

Lightly drawn pencil lines will suggest wood siding or shingles.

Many models can be dressed up with a thin decorative molding like this.

Gluing thin strips of cardboard along the corners of a house will sometimes give the model a more finished look.

Windows come in many different sizes and styles. The trim on top and bottom can get quite fancy.

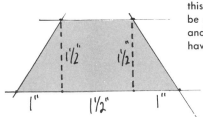

The dormer is cut out like this. The proportions can be altered to fit the size and style of house you have built.

Score along the dotted lines.

The window itself can be made separately and fitted into the dormer opening.

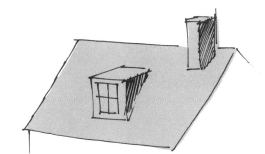

A dormer window or two will relieve the boredom of a large plain roof.

Bits of cardboard can be glued onto a long thin strip to make decorative moldings like this.

The appearance of any window will be greatly improved if you can somehow suggest the window panes. If the windows are fairly large, you can cut very thin strips of cardboard and glue them into the window opening.

Pieces of straw from a broom are more delicate and more realistic. You can fit them into the window opening or else cut them longer and glue them onto the back (inside) of the window.

If you want to suggest glass, you might cut out some thin, transparent plastic and glue it on the inside of the wall, behind the window.

4. PALACES, CASTLES, AND SUCH

The houses we've described so far can be seen almost anywhere, except perhaps in large cities. But there are all kinds of other elegant and unusual buildings that are suitable for model making. There are abbeys, cathedrals, palaces, châteaus, temples, mosques, and many historic buildings—usually built with great care and attention to detail and without much thought of costs.

Most of these buildings are so complicated they can't be very well copied exactly. But you can simplify, change around parts, concentrate on those aspects that are most interesting.

Remember that a model building doesn't have to be built in one piece. If you work in small, easy-to-handle sections, then join them together, the task will be much easier.

This is a quite accurate model of a sixth-century Byzantine church. The roof can be removed to show the interior. A model this complicated takes a good deal of time, patience, and planning if it is to turn out well. It is also important to have some good photographs or plans of the original building to refer to. Like many ambitious models, this one consists of a number of smaller sections fitted together. The model is made entirely of cardboard.

Here is a medieval castle. The notches on the upper walls are called crenelations. The defending soldiers shoot their arrows through the spaces.

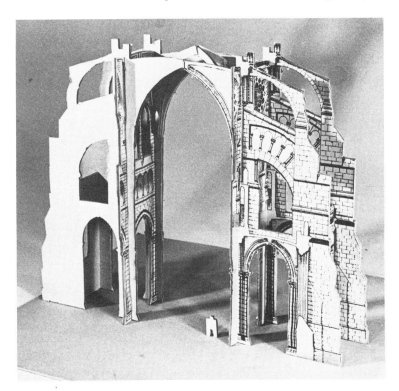

This is a cross section of a cathedral intended to show the various columns and supports involved in its construction. Something like this would make a nice stage set.

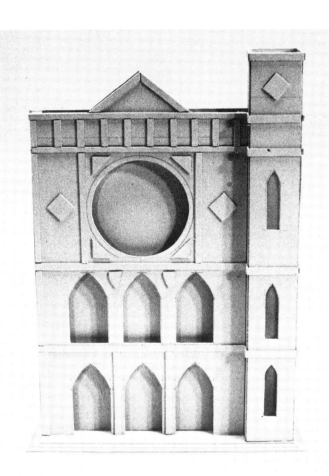

This is the facade, or front wall, of a church. Notice how the cardboard has been arranged so that there is a slight space between the different planes. This produces strong shadows in the windows.

You can see here how a column can be formed by making closely spaced score marks. This was rather heavy, stiff cardboard, so the score marks cut almost halfway through. The center arch requires careful bending and some accurate fitting.

The photograph above shows the many small parts which were assembled in different ways to make the groupings shown below and on the facing page. The arrangements shown here make little town squares or courtyards. But, working this way, with different shapes and sizes, it is possible to build a single large castle, a palace, an office building, a stadium, or whatever ambitious structure interests you.

40

41

5. HOW TO BE AN ARCHITECT

An architect who designs a house for a family (or a building for a business or industry) must keep a great many things in mind. He or she must know the number of people who are to use the building, how and where they will spend their time, how they come and go, what their needs are, the kinds of things they like to do in their spare time.

It can be great fun to design and build a model of the sort of house you would like to have for yourself, or to live in with your family. As long as it is only a model that you are making, you can ignore annoying problems like how much the house will actually cost to build, what materials are practical, or what are the limitations of the site where the house is to stand. (If you feel like being practical, you can give these matters some thought. They are enormously important when it comes to planning a house that will really be built.)

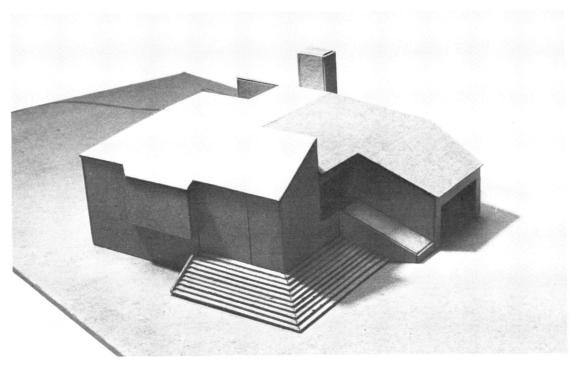

This model was built by a highly skilled professional architect. In this study he was trying out the proportions and placement of the various parts of the building. Doors, windows, and little details were not included because the main concern was with shapes and form.

This model is made up of three separate sections. One part is the living room; one is bedrooms; and the other is kitchen, bathroom, and utilities.

SCALE

In order to design your house with some realism you should have some idea of scale. Scale means the proportion of a model to the real finished building. If, for example, you work with a scale of 1 inch equals 1 foot, this means that each inch in your model represents 1 foot in the actual, full-size building. A wall that is 4 inches high in your model would be 4 *feet* high if actually built.

If you work with a scale of ½ inch equals 1 foot, a wall that is 2 inches high in the model will be 4 feet high in the full-size house.

Professional architects take great pains with scale. Their blueprints and models are always extremely accurate, so that carpenters and masons know exactly what to do and there is no chance of mistakes or misfits. We, however, can afford to be a little less fussy because it is not too likely that anyone will use the models we build as the basis for full-scale construction.

At the same time you can't totally ignore this business of scale. If you do, you may discover that the kitchen you planned won't have room for a stove or refrigerator, or that the bedroom turns out to be smaller than the bathroom. Keep a ruler handy to check sizes as you design your model, and you will end up with a more realistic-looking house. Of course you may not care a bit about realism. Then you can completely ignore this whole business of scale and just do whatever looks good to you.

When an architect has the job of planning a group of several buildings, or a building located on an unusual piece of land, he or she will often make a model that

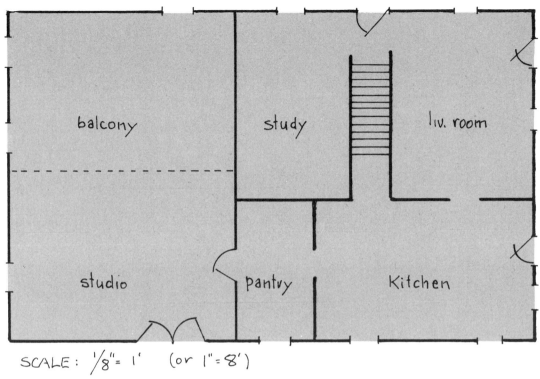

SCALE: 1/8" = 1'   (or 1" = 8')

Above is a floor plan for a house. It is the sort of preliminary plan an architect would draw. It tells the exact size of each area and locates doors, windows, walls, stairs, and so on. A large office building may require hundreds of blueprints such as this, showing everything from main supporting beams and columns to such small details as how and where a doorknob is to be placed. A side view of a building (below) is called an elevation.

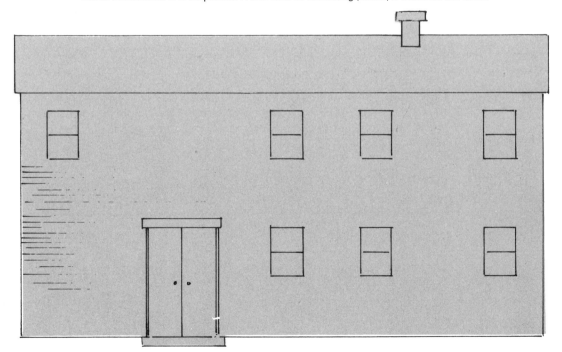

shows the surrounding landscape. This gives a better idea of what the finished construction will look like when placed in its setting. As you can see, this kind of a model can get complicated and may require weeks and months of very careful building.

In this model you can see the planned office building, its parking lot, the neighboring houses and street, trees, sidewalks, and how the land itself is shaped.

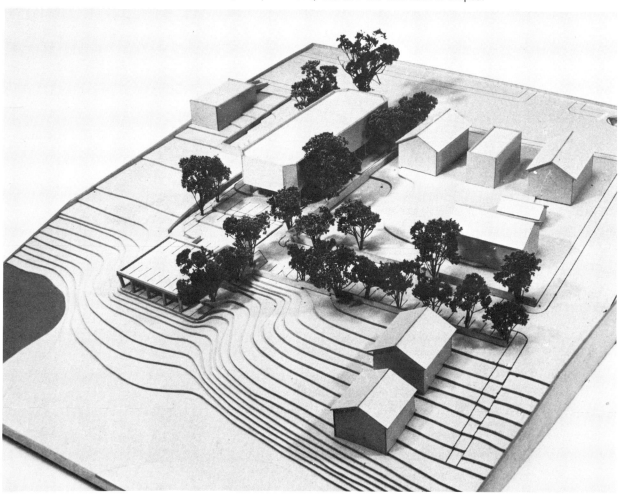

An architecture student built this enormously complicated model, only a section of which is shown in the photograph. The problem was to design a series of school buildings on an already existing pier. Some of the roofs have been left uncovered to show construction details.

This model was trying out a rather unusual window arrangement. The little cut-out figure on the right serves to give a sense of scale. Notice the small weather vane on the roof.

MODEL BUILDINGS
OF WOOD

6. USING WOOD

It takes a little time and effort to make a model house of wood. You first have to hunt about to find the right kind of wood. You then have to cut and sandpaper with care and patience. But the results will be worth it, because wood is a handsome material and your finished building will have a strong, permanent look. You can also make it quite a bit larger than a cardboard house.

WHAT KIND OF WOOD TO USE?

Balsa Wood This kind of wood is sometimes used for model-house construction. It is lightweight and easy to cut. In fact, you can handle it almost as if it were cardboard. A sharp, pointy knife will cut through it. (You can't, however, score and bend it like cardboard.) It can be bought in any hobby shop in various sizes and thicknesses. The best thickness for model-house building is about ¹/₁₆ inch. There are two disadvantages. One is that balsa wood is delicate and not very strong. It must be handled with care or it will split. The other disadvantage is that it is quite expensive.

Lattice Wood   Lumber yards sell a ¼-inch thick wood which comes in long strips. It is called lattice wood. It is available in various widths from about ¾ inch wide up to 3 inches wide. An 8-foot long strip of this wood, 1½ inches wide, will cost less than a dollar and will provide a good part of the material required for a fair-sized house.

Here are a few strips of lattice wood in various widths.

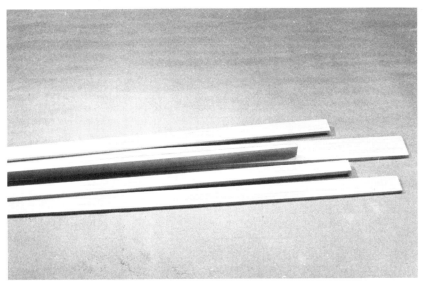

The model on page 48 was built with lattice wood, as was the house in the next chapter. Lattice wood has no knots or rough grain and the edges are straight and clean, so that the glue sticks well. Lattice wood is strong. It is good looking. It is easy to work with. And perhaps, most important, if you use the method of construction shown in the next chapter, you can entirely avoid the rather messy business of cutting out windows and doors. If you can possibly get this kind of wood, by all means do so.

Plywood   This might seem like the best material for our purposes. But not so. It is difficult to cut, and the edges have a tendency to split and splinter. The surface of common plywood is often unpleasant with a conspicuous grain. It is tricky to cut doors and windows from it. You can use it if nothing else is available, but the results won't be quite the same as with the other kinds of wood.

There is a time, however, when you will want to use plywood. And that is when the model building you want to construct is large. Dollhouses, for example, are often built with plywood because they are usually quite a bit bigger than the houses described in the next three chapters.

Other Kinds Of Wood   There are many other kinds of thin wood which may be easy for you to get and which you can use. Some of the crates used to hold fruits and vegetables have sides made of thin wood slats, or you might be lucky enough to find the kind of solid wood box that expensive cigars come in, which is a smooth dark-brown cedar. If you know somebody who has the use of a woodworking shop, see if you can get him to cut you some thin strips from the edge of boards.

Some hobby shops carry wide strips of a very good-looking wood called basswood. It is smooth and much stronger than balsa. But, because the wood is strong, it is not easy to cut out doors and windows. After you've had some experience constructing a few buildings, you might want to try basswood. It can be very useful in combination with other kinds of wood.

THE TOOLS

The most important tool is a saw. It should have many small teeth. A straight-back saw like the one shown here

will work fine. There is also a very small, sharp little saw that is specially made for model work. It is called a razor saw. It is very thin, and it will fit into an X-Acto tool handle. It will cost about two dollars and is very useful. A hacksaw blade will work well, if it is new and sharp. The saw you want to avoid using is one of the large, coarse-toothed kind intended for rough carpentry. Its blade won't cut a thin piece of board without a lot of splintering and jagged edges. A file will also come in handy.

The other tool you should have is a square. This will let you rule a straight line squarely across a piece of wood. Without a straight line to guide you, it is hard to make a true right-angle cut. A miter box is another device that lets you cut squarely across a strip of wood. It holds the saw at right angles to the wood. If you can't find a square or a miter box, you can use a box or the edges of a book to rule a line truly across your wood.

This is a miter box with a saw. The saw fits into the slots and cuts a piece of wood either straight across, or at a 45-degree angle—depending on which slots are used.

White glue, such as Elmer's or Sobo, works well. Always read the label on any other kind of glue to make sure it is intended for wood and is fast drying.

You'll also need plenty of sandpaper. Get a few sheets of medium roughness and a few of fine.

7. BUILDING A TOWN HOUSE

The houses on these pages may look to you like quite difficult undertakings. They aren't at all, though they do require a bit of time and some patience. You won't be able to complete one in an afternoon.

Model buildings like these are not hard to make if the wood-strip method is used. For this, you will need the kind of lattice-wood strips mentioned in the previous pages. The strips are glued edge to edge. A window or door is made by simply leaving out a section of the lattice strip wherever you want an opening. In this way the difficult job of cutting out these openings is completely avoided. With little effort you are sure of a square, neat door or window, without any uneven or jagged edges.

The walls are built one at a time while laid flat on a table. Then the four walls are stood up vertically and glued together. Finally, the roof and additional details are added.

Our partly finished house with the "heavy construction" completed is shown here. The walls and roof have been assembled, and the garage is partly done. This photograph shows clearly how the strips of lattice wood have been glued edge to edge to form the walls, windows, and a door.

The house shown here is a sort that can be found in many places and in many variations all over the world. As the name implies, though, it is most often found in towns and cities. If you want to make a different kind of house, you can simply change the sizes and proportions given here. You could make an old farmhouse, a modern split-level, a ranch house, or a tall narrow tenement.

The materials needed to make the model described on the next few pages are two 8-foot strips of lattice wood 1¼ inches wide, and two 8-foot strips 1 inch wide. (The actual finished size of the wood you get from the lumber yard will be about ⅛ inch narrower. The size you order is the size *before* the wood is planed and sanded smooth.) On the models shown in the photographs, odd scraps of thin oak or mahogany were used for some of the details, such as door and window trim.

METHOD OF CONSTRUCTION

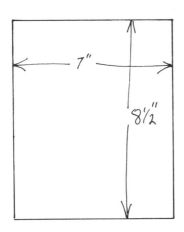

1. Get a piece of typewriter paper or stationery, or use a sheet of paper from a drawing pad. Measure up from the bottom 8½ inches, and in from one side 7 inches, as shown. Make sure these lines are straight and parallel to the edges of the paper. This sheet of paper is used as a sort of plan or pattern for the walls. All corners will be at right angles and all sides will be parallel. When you use it as a guide, you can be fairly

If you are unable to get lattice wood to work with, and have only plywood, see page 89, which explains how doors and windows are cut out of this material.

sure that the walls of the house will stand up straight when they are attached to one another. (You can sketch in the windows and doors if you want, though this is not really necessary.)

2. Put your "plan" on the table where you are going to work. You must have a surface with no bumps or unevennesses. Lay a piece of clear plastic kitchen wrap over the plan. This is to keep the glue from sticking to the plan.

3. Cut a strip of lattice 8½ inches long. Use the 1-inch wide wood. Lay it down over your plan (on top of the clear plastic kitchen wrap) along the left-hand side.

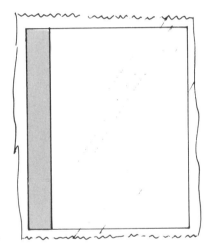

4. Cut three short pieces, as shown. Use the 1¼-inch lattice wood for these. If the edges are rough, sand them smooth. It is easier to do the sanding now than later. Apply glue and attach to the first strip. Hold them tight up against the first strip for a minute or two until the glue has a chance to set.

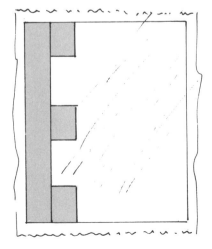

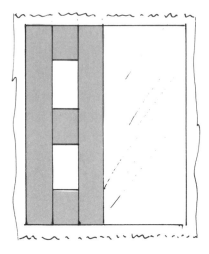

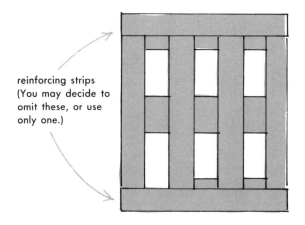

reinforcing strips
(You may decide to
omit these, or use
only one.)

5. Cut another 8½-inch strip of the narrower wood, and attach it with glue to the three short pieces. Now you have a piece of the front wall with two windows!

6. Continue cutting and gluing strips together until the entire wall is completed. Make sure that all the full-length strips are the same size. To make a door on a wall, omit the short, lower right-hand piece.

7. Allow the glue to set for at least a half hour. Then carefully pick up the wall, peel off the clear plastic kitchen wrap, and scrape off any glue that may have oozed onto the back of the wall.

8. At this point the wall will be quite fragile, but if you now turn the wall face-down and cut and glue on two strips as shown, the wall will become strong and rigid.

9. The rear wall can be made next, and it is made the same way as the front wall unless you want to change the placement of the windows somewhat. You might,

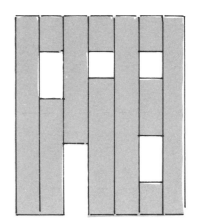

for example, want to have fewer windows in the back or windows of a somewhat different size. And the back door might be put in a different place.

10. The two side walls are made by this same method. But your house will look more interesting if the side walls are a little longer or else shorter than the front and back ones. A building that is perfectly square doesn't usually look as good as one that is rectangular. You can easily alter the width of a wall by either adding or removing some of the lattice-wood strips to suit your own ideas. The windows don't have to be exactly even or the placement the same on all four walls. A little variety in their arrangement will add a lot of interest.

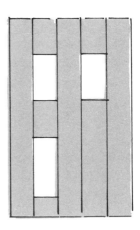

11. Glue reinforcing strips along the inside of the side walls as shown. When you cut these strips make them ½ inch less wide than the wall itself. Then position them ¼ inch in from each end of the wall. This will allow the side

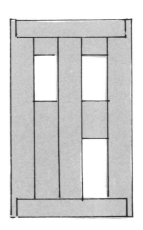

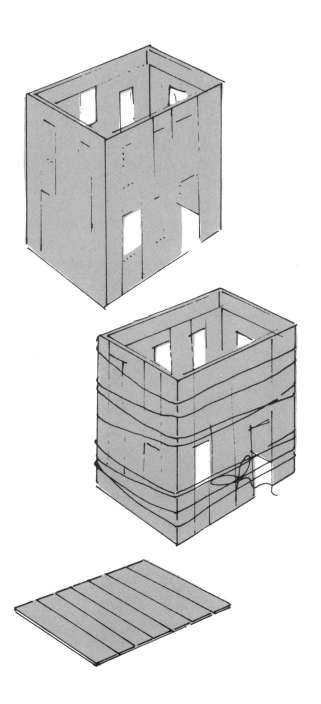

walls to fit in snugly against the front and back walls.

12. Temporarily assemble all the walls to make sure everything goes neatly and tightly together. If there is a corner that isn't quite square, or if the bottom doesn't sit evenly on a flat surface, make any needed corrections. Some filing or sandpapering at this time usually can correct an edge that doesn't fit or a wobbly bottom.

13. Apply glue to the corners and put the walls together. Wrap the model with string to keep the walls tight until the glue dries. This will take at least half an hour—longer, if you have used a lot of glue. If you think your model needs a little extra reinforcement, glue small blocks of wood in the corners.

14. You can make the roof next. A flat roof is the easiest to make. Several lattice strips glued edge to edge will do the trick.

This completes the basic house. If you have used the method described here, you will have a model like the one shown below. (If you have changed the proportions, you will have something quite different. There's nothing wrong with that!) On the next two pages are some photographs taken as our model was being built. And the next chapter explains how the model can be elaborated and improved in a number of different ways.

This is the same model house shown on page 57. But it has a flat roof at this time.

Here are some photographs showing the basic steps in assembling one wall using the method described on the preceding pages. The lower-right photograph shows a reinforcing strip. It is being held in place with spring clothespins while the glue dries.

The four walls have been assembled, and a few stout rubber bands are holding everything together until the glue has dried.

The walls shown here are for the town house pictured on page 48. The lattice strips are assembled in a way that is a little different from the method shown in this chapter because the arrangement of windows and doors was being experimented with.

8. ADDING MORE DETAIL

THE TRIM

The thin stripping around doors and windows is called the trim, and it adds a great deal of realism to any model building. On some of the buildings shown here it is also used as decoration to keep a wall from looking too plain or monotonous. In some styles of buildings the trim is carved or notched and can be quite elaborate. The difficult part of this operation is getting suitable material for the stripping. There are several possibilities: (1) Get thin sheets of balsa wood (about ⅛ inch thick) and with a sharp knife cut the strips to the width you want. A pointy model-maker's knife or a utility knife is best for this job. You will also need a metal ruler to guide the blade as you cut. (2) Cardboard is another possibility. If it is cut accu-

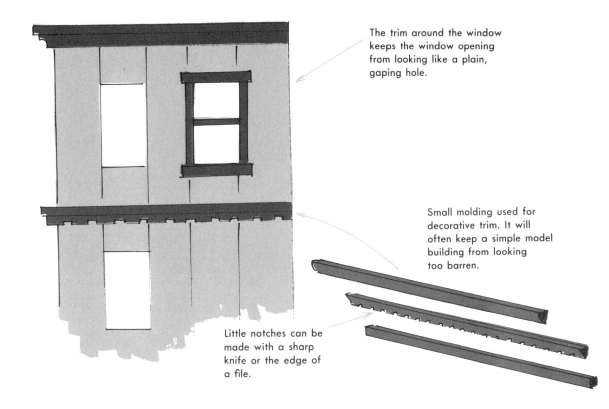

The trim around the window keeps the window opening from looking like a plain, gaping hole.

Small molding used for decorative trim. It will often keep a simple model building from looking too barren.

Little notches can be made with a sharp knife or the edge of a file.

rately it will look quite nice. (3) You may be able to get somebody with a woodworking shop to cut some strips using power tools.

Several of the model buildings illustrated have trim cut from mahogany, which is a dark wood. This makes a very nice contrast with the light-colored pine lattice wood. You can also paint the trim to make it a different color from the rest of the house. Do the painting before the trim is put in place. It will make a much neater job.

The trim is simply cut to size and attached with glue. Accuracy and care are important if you want it to look good.

The model from the previous chapter has been given a little bell tower—without a bell as yet. Thin strips of wood—the trim—have been placed around windows and doors. In this model the strips seem a little heavier than need be. The trim used in the model below looks a bit neater.

This close-up view shows the use of some decorative molding. You can also see how nice stairs look when set in place.

ROOFS

There are many different kinds of roofs—most of them more interesting than a plain, flat roof. And most of them are somewhat tricky to make. The drawings here show a few of the possibilities.

This is an easy type of roof to make.

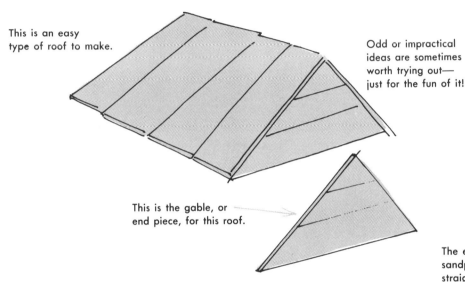

Odd or impractical ideas are sometimes worth trying out—just for the fun of it!

This is the gable, or end piece, for this roof.

The edges should be filed and sandpapered until they are straight and even.

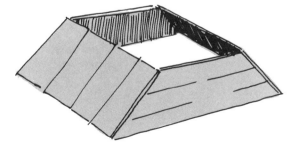

This is the sort of roof used on the model shown on page 48. A flat piece of wood on top finishes it off.

Roofs of this sort are often used on barns.

Here is a quite complicated roof in the course of construction. There are two dormers and a little six-sided window. A lot of patient cutting and fitting and refitting are involved in a roof with so many different angles.

PORCHES AND OTHER DETAILS

Porches and balconies will make any house a lot more interesting. In most cases you will have to add a base to the house in order to have a place where the balcony or porch supports can be attached.

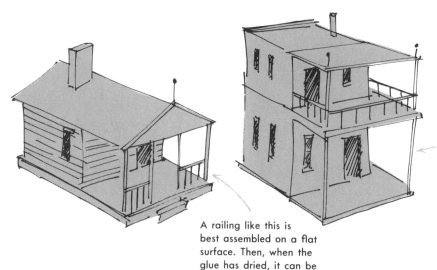

Wood matchsticks, bamboo strips, coat-hanger wire, or any thin, stiff material can be used for railings.

Thin wood rods, called applicator sticks, can be obtained at most drugstores. They make excellent railings and supports for porches.

A railing like this is best assembled on a flat surface. Then, when the glue has dried, it can be stood up and put in place.

There is no one way or correct way to make porches and railings. Some model buildings can be improved with this sort of addition; on some buildings it serves no practical purpose.

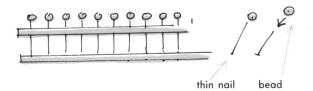

thin nail   bead

All sorts of odd and miscellaneous materials can be used to add interesting little details to a model house. For example, the railing along the roof of the town house on page 48 uses thin nails set in a row with little beads glued onto the ends. The assembled railing was then given several coats of white paint.

Small decorative details of various sorts can be cut from strips of wood. Round shapes can be made by cutting slices from a wood dowel or old broomstick handle.

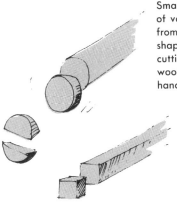

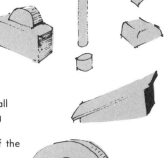

It is usually easier to build up a complicated shape by glueing together separate small parts, rather than by whittling the shape out of a single large block of wood. Some of the more ornate buildings in the next chapter use a lot of small objects of this sort.

Arches like this can be easily made with a round file.

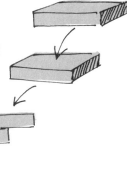

Short pieces of lattice wood can be glued together like this to make a staircase.

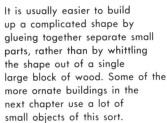

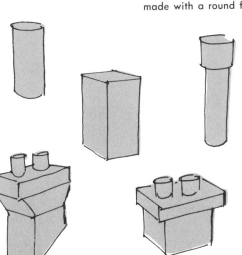

Chimneys can be anything from a simple little square on a cottage roof to a quite elaborate construction suitable for a French château.

9. SOME OTHER WOOD BUILDINGS

In this chapter there are photographs and drawings of a variety of model wood buildings—some realistic and practical, some completely fanciful and impractical. They are not included so that you can copy them—although you could if you wanted to. Rather, they are intended to show various ideas for buildings and different ways of working. And they show several ways of using wood as well as other materials. You may find that some of the methods of construction will be useful when you set out to design and build a masterpiece of your own.

A PALACE

The very fancy-looking building on the opposite page is actually one building inside another. The inner building is a simple construction using lattice wood for the

corners and cross pieces. The outer building, however, gets a little more complicated. It uses quite a few ¼-inch dowels. Dowels are wood rods that can be bought for a few cents at any lumberyard or hardware store. They come in 3-foot lengths and are available in sizes from ⅛-inch to 1-inch diameter. They are extremely useful for all kinds of model building.

Here is another structure, not unlike the one on the previous page. In this case, however, the separate parts are attached one on top of another to make a tall, narrow tower.

This little house was made in Puerto Rico, using a type of stiff reed that grows there.

A MODERN HOUSE

Many modern houses use a great deal of glass. And this partly finished model house is no exception. Instead of glass, which may be hard to get in the sizes you want, you can use a heavy, clear plastic. The outside of the house has also been treated in a different way. It was given a sand texture to make it look like concrete. The sand texture can be easily made. Paint a heavy layer of glue onto the walls while they are in a horizontal position. Then sprinkle on a handful of fine sand. Let the glue harden for a half hour or so. Then shake off the extra sand. You can use this same method with other materials beside sand. Sawdust, feathers, ashes, or any similar material can be used.

A FACADE

A facade (pronounced "fa-sod") is the front of a building. There may be situations where this is the only part of a building that you want to make. This might well be the case with something as elaborate as a church or cathedral or a royal palace. To make a model of very large, complicated structures like these requires more time and patience than most of us can muster.

However, a facade, or front "slice," can give a pretty good idea of the style and character of the original. (Besides, it can be hung on a wall and look quite elegant.)

The facade shown here is made from lattice wood glued together horizontally. Thin strips of wood with notches and some odd and miscellaneous pieces of wood from the scrap box are placed here and there for decoration.

CONSTRUCTION MODELS

Sometimes a wood model building is made for the pleasure of trying out unusual methods of construction. The partly built model shown below is of a Japanese temple; such structures were built with ingeniously designed interlocking joints and notches. When the model is finished, it will be roofed with woven bamboo screening.

The model on the next page was a school design problem. The object was to show all the construction details for a small garden shelter. Models like these, if neatly and accurately done, are almost like blueprints, and can serve as a guide to the construction of the actual, full-scale building.

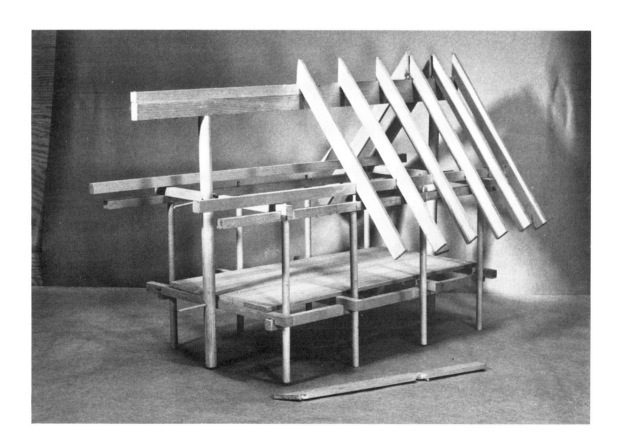

These photographs show a small garden shelter. Below, the model is turned on its side to show the location of columns and beams.

This model is based on the kind of commercial building erected in many cities during the 1900's.

Here are a few drawings of a variety of buildings. They may give you ideas. If you do decide to make a model of a historic building, you should get some books with good clear photographs or drawings that you can refer to.

10. DOLLHOUSES

A dollhouse is in many ways just like the model wood buildings already described. But there are three ways in which it is quite different: (1) It is fairly large. (2) It must be easy to open up—or have one side with no walls so that you can see what goes on inside. (3) It should be furnished.

In other words, the *inside* of a dollhouse is more important than the outside. But, even so, you don't want to build something with a rough and sloppy exterior. The nicest kind of dollhouse is carefully built inside and out.

Because dollhouses are large, plywood is a more suitable material to use than wood lattice strips. Plywood comes in different thicknesses, measuring from ¼ inch up to ¾ inch. The ¼-inch size is best for the average, not too huge dollhouse.

If you can't get plywood, you can make do with several

Here is a handsome, completely finished dollhouse. It takes a lot of time and effort to achieve this kind of detail.

There are many ways of opening up a dollhouse. In the one shown here and on the opposite page, the roof is on hinges and can be raised. The front wall is also hinged and can be swung open like a door. This particular dollhouse is commercially produced, using a very smooth, nice-looking plywood. It seems a little barren at the moment, but eventually it will look quite different with the windows and door finished off and all the interior completed.

other materials such as wood boards, various kinds of particle board or hardboard, or even heavy cardboard if it is reinforced with strips of wood.

The plans on the next page are for a flat-roofed house, which is the easiest kind to build. (It is really a little like a big box.) All the main parts—roof, floors, walls—have straight, right-angled sides, so that they can be easily cut. Or you can have them cut for you by somebody with a power saw, or at the lumberyard.

The plans are designed on a scale of 1 inch equals 1 foot. Most dollhouses are built to this scale, as are most commercially manufactured accessories, such as chairs, tables, and beds. If, however, you have some ideas of your own and want to change the sizes or proportions, by all means do so.

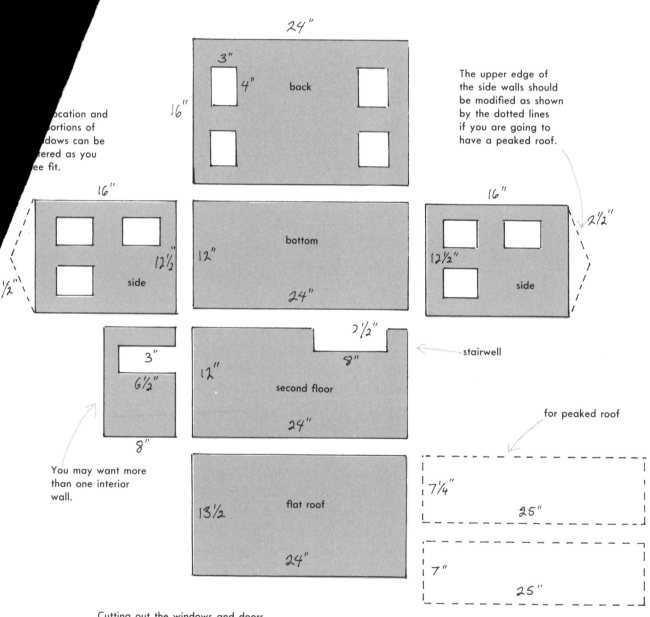

24"

3"

4" back

16"

location and
portions of
windows can be
tered as you
ee fit.

The upper edge of
the side walls should
be modified as shown
by the dotted lines
if you are going to
have a peaked roof.

16"

16"

2½"

2½"

12½"

side

12" bottom

24"

12½"

side

2½"

3"

6½"

8"

You may want more
than one interior
wall.

2½"

stairwell

12"

8"

second floor

24"

for peaked roof

13½ flat roof

24"

7¼"

25"

7"

25"

Cutting out the windows and doors
can be tricky. See pages 88 and 89.

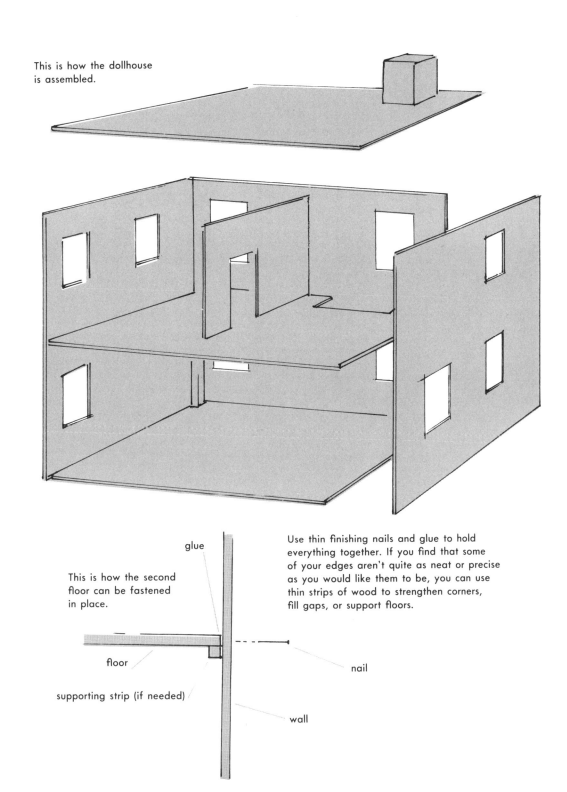

This is how the dollhouse is assembled.

This is how the second floor can be fastened in place.

glue

floor

supporting strip (if needed)

nail

wall

Use thin finishing nails and glue to hold everything together. If you find that some of your edges aren't quite as neat or precise as you would like them to be, you can use thin strips of wood to strengthen corners, fill gaps, or support floors.

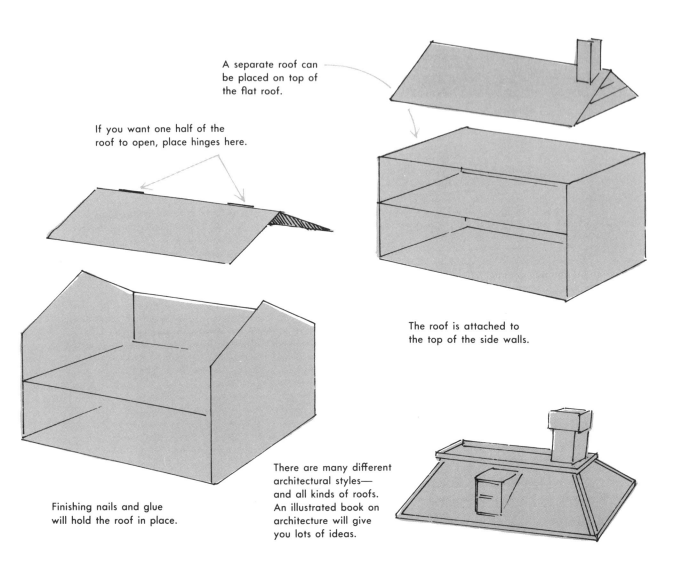

A separate roof can be placed on top of the flat roof.

If you want one half of the roof to open, place hinges here.

The roof is attached to the top of the side walls.

Finishing nails and glue will hold the roof in place.

There are many different architectural styles—and all kinds of roofs. An illustrated book on architecture will give you lots of ideas.

The only difficult part of building a dollhouse is cutting out the windows and doors. If you find that this job is more than you can handle, you might want to settle for painted-on windows. Use a light blue color to look like glass and glue on thin strips of wood for the trim. If you are going to cut out the windows and doors, follow the steps shown opposite.

CUTTING OUT WINDOWS AND DOORS

1. With a pencil and ruler carefully mark the locations of all the openings you want to make.

2. Drill a hole in one corner. The hole must be large enough to permit a narrow saw blade to pass through. (If you can't drill a large enough hole, drill two holes as close together as possible. Then with a knife, cut a gap to connect them.)

two connected holes

3. Put your saw blade through the hole and cut along the two sides of the window, as shown.

A saw like this, called a keyhole saw, will do the job. If you have nothing else, a sharp hacksaw blade can be used.

4. Drill another hole in the corner opposite and repeat the above step.

5. With a file, go over the edges and get rid of all the bumps and irregularities. Finish off with sandpaper.

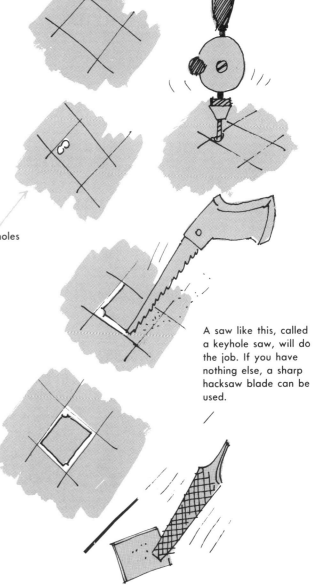

Here is a large, quite elaborate dollhouse which is simply left open in the back. The door and one window have been finished off.

There are several possible ways of making the inside of a dollhouse accessible. The easiest way is to simply omit the back wall—or the front wall if you prefer. A better way, though somewhat more complicated, is to have the front wall hinged. Then you can open out or close up your dollhouse as you see fit.

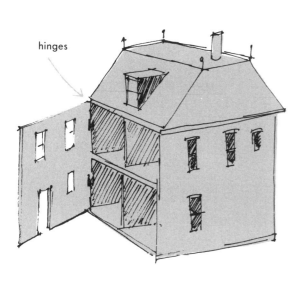

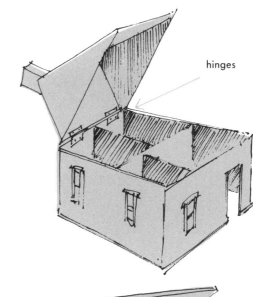

Dolhouses can be many things beside plain country or suburban homes. You might want to make a Colorado mining-town saloon, an adobe dwelling, an Austrian palace, or any other kind of building that interests you. Most dollhouses, in actual fact, have nothing at all to do with dolls—despite the name. They are more concerned with small-scale interior decoration!

The dollhouse shown here is really a horse house, or if you prefer, a stable. Half the roof can be removed for a better view of the interior. This is just the sort of thing for people who prefer horses to people!

This is a close-up view of the door and window on the house shown on page 90. These parts are commercially produced separately and intended to fit onto a standard, store-bought dollhouse, and needless to say, they are very expensive. (The window actually slides up and down.) The dollhouse below has a lot of exterior detail. There are shutters, window boxes, and a large, good-looking porch.

Here is the back view of the house shown in the lower photograph on the previous page. Notice the fireplaces and the steps.

A dollhouse with a bare, unadorned exterior will always look unfinished . . . even if the inside is carefully decorated. So give some thought to the trim around windows and doors, to railings, shutters, decorative moldings, and so on. The details discussed in Chapter 8 can be used with any dollhouse.

Dollhouse furniture and interior decoration can be a very elaborate business, and they are certainly highly important. But they are also a matter beyond the scope

This is the interior of the dollhouse shown on page 83. It has been designed with great skill, patience, and good taste. It is amazingly complete, with no detail overlooked. It is even wired with tiny electric lights so that it can be illuminated at night.

of this book. You should have no trouble, however, finding bits of wallpaper and scraps of rug and cloth to decorate floors, walls, and windows. Chairs, tables, and all the various things that fill a house can be made from scraps of wood, or bought in toy or hobby shops.

ABOUT THE AUTHOR

Harvey Weiss has written and illustrated many books for children. A distinguished sculptor, whose work has received many awards and has been exhibited in galleries and museums across the country, Mr. Weiss brings to his books a sure sense of what appeals to and can be accomplished by young people, and a sculptor's eye for simple, uncluttered forms.

A dedicated tinkerer and gadgeteer, he has exercised his considerable and varied skills on such projects as an elegant model railroad world, a wholly impractical, very complicated steam-powered model airplane, and a large model tugboat, also steam-powered. Mr. Weiss first began to put together model buildings a number of years ago as part of a model railroad landscape. As he worked on them, he found that they often developed a distinctive character of their own, apart from their role in a setting for trains. Soon he found himself making, simply for their own sake, larger, more fanciful and elaborate structures. He often wishes he had the time and space to build an entire town, or at least a city block, of model buildings.

Mr. Weiss is professor of sculpture at Adelphi University and lives in Greens Farms, Connecticut.